Hope you enjoy your stay.

Please sign our guest book.

Thank you.

DATE	NAME

COMMENT:

DATE	NAME

COMMENT:

DATE	NAME

COMMENT:

DATE

NAME

COMMENT:

DATE

NAME

COMMENT:

DATE

NAME

COMMENT:

DATE	NAME

COMMENT:

DATE	NAME

COMMENT:

DATE	NAME

COMMENT:

DATE

NAME

COMMENT:

DATE

NAME

COMMENT:

DATE

NAME

COMMENT:

DATE	NAME

COMMENT:

DATE	NAME

COMMENT:

DATE	NAME

COMMENT:

DATE	NAME

COMMENT:

DATE	NAME

COMMENT:

DATE	NAME

COMMENT:

DATE

NAME

COMMENT:

DATE

NAME

COMMENT:

DATE

NAME

COMMENT:

DATE	NAME

COMMENT:

DATE	NAME

COMMENT:

DATE	NAME

COMMENT:

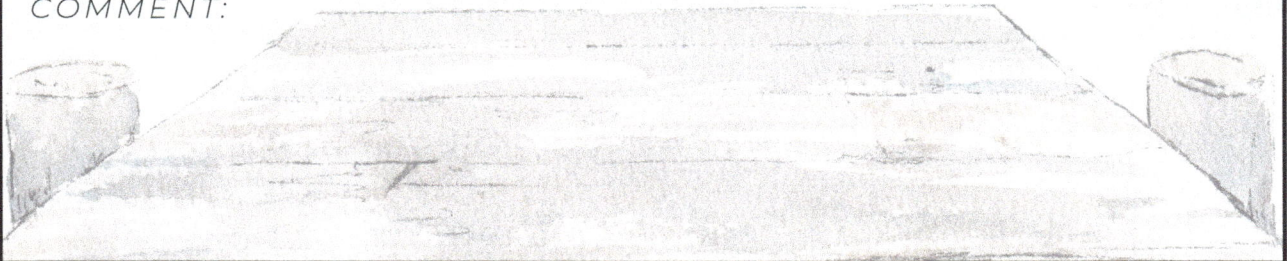

DATE	NAME

COMMENT:

DATE	NAME

COMMENT:

DATE	NAME

COMMENT:

DATE	NAME

COMMENT:

DATE	NAME

COMMENT:

DATE	NAME

COMMENT:

DATE

NAME

COMMENT:

DATE

NAME

COMMENT:

DATE

NAME

COMMENT:

DATE	NAME

COMMENT:

DATE	NAME

COMMENT:

DATE	NAME

COMMENT:

DATE

NAME

COMMENT:

DATE

NAME

COMMENT:

DATE

NAME

COMMENT:

DATE	NAME

COMMENT:

DATE	NAME

COMMENT:

DATE	NAME

COMMENT:

DATE	NAME

COMMENT:

DATE	NAME

COMMENT:

DATE	NAME

COMMENT:

DATE

NAME

COMMENT:

DATE

NAME

COMMENT:

DATE

NAME

COMMENT:

DATE	NAME

COMMENT:

DATE	NAME

COMMENT:

DATE	NAME

COMMENT:

DATE	NAME

COMMENT:

DATE	NAME

COMMENT:

DATE	NAME

COMMENT:

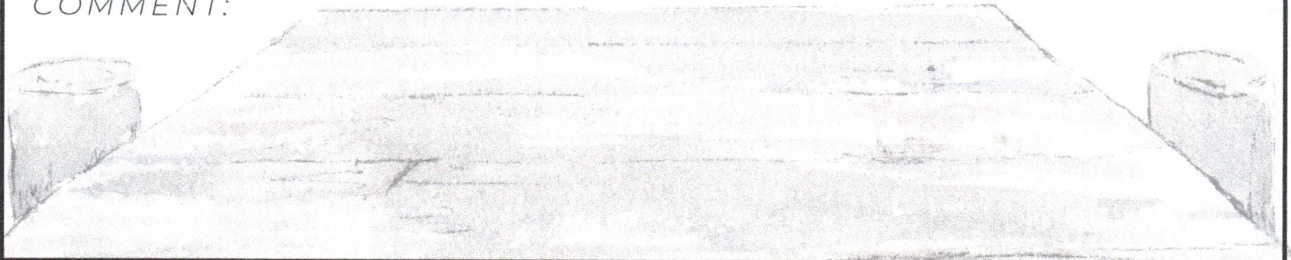

DATE

NAME

COMMENT:

DATE

NAME

COMMENT:

DATE

NAME

COMMENT:

DATE	NAME

COMMENT:

DATE	NAME

COMMENT:

DATE	NAME

COMMENT:

DATE

NAME

COMMENT:

DATE

NAME

COMMENT:

DATE

NAME

COMMENT:

DATE	NAME

COMMENT:

DATE	NAME

COMMENT:

DATE	NAME

COMMENT:

DATE

NAME

COMMENT:

DATE

NAME

COMMENT:

DATE

NAME

COMMENT:

DATE

NAME

COMMENT:

DATE

NAME

COMMENT:

DATE

NAME

COMMENT:

DATE	NAME

COMMENT:

DATE	NAME

COMMENT:

DATE	NAME

COMMENT:

DATE	NAME

COMMENT:

DATE	NAME

COMMENT:

DATE	NAME

COMMENT:

DATE	NAME

COMMENT:

DATE	NAME

COMMENT:

DATE	NAME

COMMENT:

DATE

NAME

COMMENT:

DATE

NAME

COMMENT:

DATE

NAME

COMMENT:

DATE	NAME

COMMENT:

DATE	NAME

COMMENT:

DATE	NAME

COMMENT:
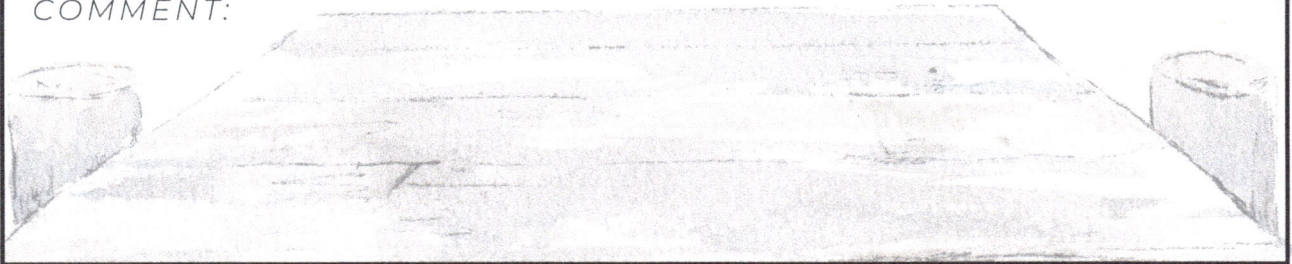

DATE

NAME

COMMENT:

DATE

NAME

COMMENT:

DATE

NAME

COMMENT:

DATE

NAME

COMMENT:

DATE

NAME

COMMENT:

DATE

NAME

COMMENT:

DATE	NAME

COMMENT:

DATE	NAME

COMMENT:

DATE	NAME

COMMENT:

DATE	NAME

COMMENT:

DATE	NAME

COMMENT:

DATE	NAME

COMMENT:

DATE	NAME

COMMENT:

DATE	NAME

COMMENT:

DATE	NAME

COMMENT:

DATE	NAME

COMMENT:

DATE	NAME

COMMENT:

DATE	NAME

COMMENT:

DATE

NAME

COMMENT:

DATE

NAME

COMMENT:

DATE

NAME

COMMENT:

DATE	NAME

COMMENT:

DATE	NAME

COMMENT:

DATE	NAME

COMMENT:

DATE	NAME

COMMENT:

DATE	NAME

COMMENT:

DATE	NAME

COMMENT:

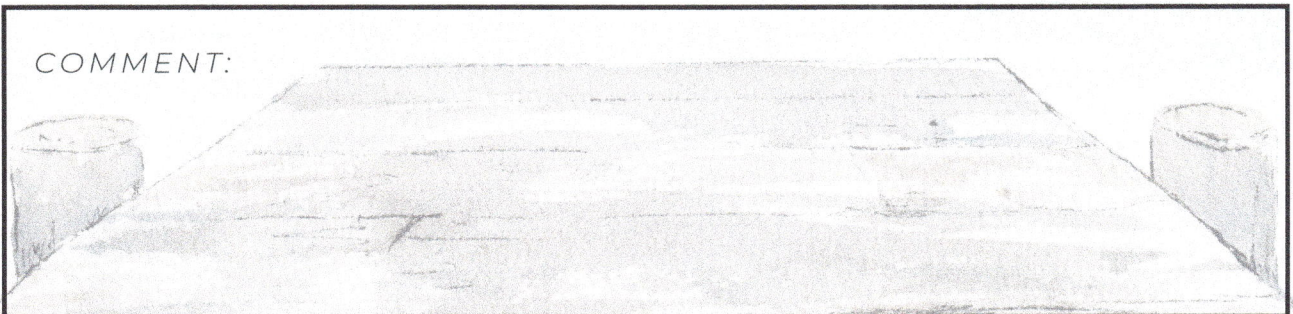

DATE	NAME

COMMENT:

DATE	NAME

COMMENT:

DATE	NAME

COMMENT:

DATE

NAME

COMMENT:

DATE

NAME

COMMENT:

DATE

NAME

COMMENT:

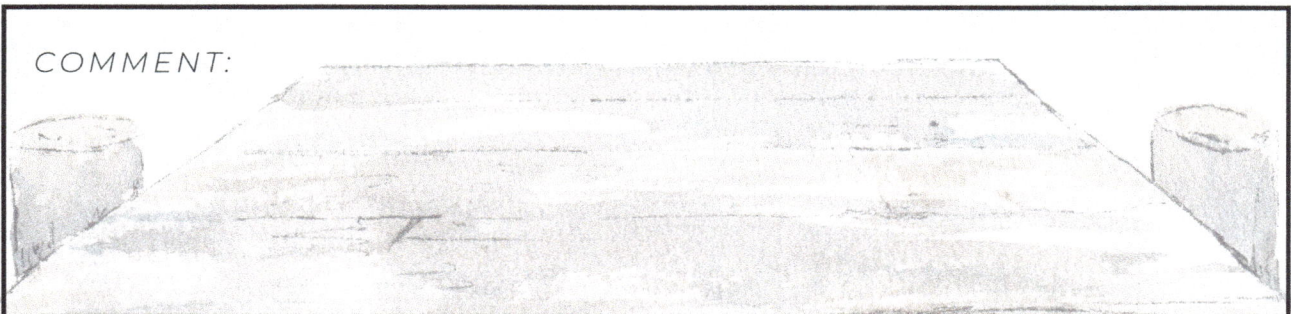

DATE

NAME

COMMENT:

DATE

NAME

COMMENT:

DATE

NAME

COMMENT:

DATE

NAME

COMMENT:

DATE

NAME

COMMENT:

DATE

NAME

COMMENT:

DATE

NAME

COMMENT:

DATE

NAME

COMMENT:

DATE

NAME

COMMENT:

DATE

NAME

COMMENT:

DATE

NAME

COMMENT:

DATE

NAME

COMMENT:

DATE	NAME

COMMENT:

DATE	NAME

COMMENT:

DATE	NAME

COMMENT:

DATE

NAME

COMMENT:

DATE

NAME

COMMENT:

DATE

NAME

COMMENT:

DATE

NAME

COMMENT:

DATE

NAME

COMMENT:

DATE

NAME

COMMENT:

DATE

NAME

COMMENT:

DATE

NAME

COMMENT:

DATE

NAME

COMMENT:

DATE	NAME

COMMENT:

DATE	NAME

COMMENT:

DATE	NAME

COMMENT:

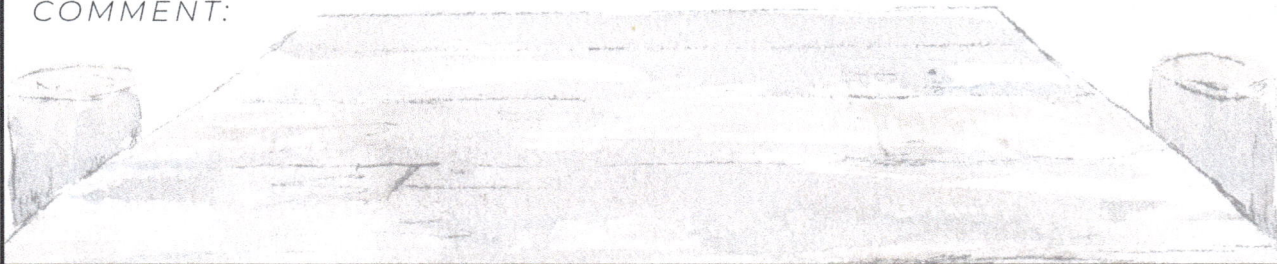

DATE

NAME

COMMENT:

DATE

NAME

COMMENT:

DATE

NAME

COMMENT:

DATE

NAME

COMMENT:

DATE

NAME

COMMENT:

DATE

NAME

COMMENT:

DATE

NAME

COMMENT:

DATE

NAME

COMMENT:

DATE

NAME

COMMENT:

DATE

NAME

COMMENT:

DATE

NAME

COMMENT:

DATE

NAME

COMMENT:

DATE	NAME

COMMENT:

DATE	NAME

COMMENT:

DATE	NAME

COMMENT:

DATE	NAME

COMMENT:

DATE	NAME

COMMENT:

DATE	NAME

COMMENT:

DATE

NAME

COMMENT:

DATE

NAME

COMMENT:

DATE

NAME

COMMENT:

DATE

NAME

COMMENT:

DATE

NAME

COMMENT:

DATE

NAME

COMMENT:

DATE

NAME

COMMENT:

DATE

NAME

COMMENT:

DATE

NAME

COMMENT:

DATE	NAME

COMMENT:

DATE	NAME

COMMENT:

DATE	NAME

COMMENT:

DATE	NAME

COMMENT:

DATE	NAME

COMMENT:

DATE	NAME

COMMENT:

DATE

NAME

COMMENT:

DATE

NAME

COMMENT:

DATE

NAME

COMMENT:

DATE

NAME

COMMENT:

DATE

NAME

COMMENT:

DATE

NAME

COMMENT:

| DATE | NAME |

COMMENT:

| DATE | NAME |

COMMENT:

| DATE | NAME |

COMMENT:

DATE

NAME

COMMENT:

DATE

NAME

COMMENT:

DATE

NAME

COMMENT:

DATE	NAME

COMMENT:

DATE	NAME

COMMENT:

DATE	NAME

COMMENT:

DATE

NAME

COMMENT:

DATE

NAME

COMMENT:

DATE

NAME

COMMENT:

DATE

NAME

COMMENT:

DATE

NAME

COMMENT:

DATE

NAME

COMMENT:

DATE

NAME

COMMENT:

DATE

NAME

COMMENT:

DATE

NAME

COMMENT:

DATE	NAME

COMMENT:

DATE	NAME

COMMENT:

DATE	NAME

COMMENT:

www.ingramcontent.com/pod-product-compliance
Lightning Source LLC
Chambersburg PA
CBHW041607260326
41914CB00012B/1409